A Comprehensive List of What
Not to Say to Black People,
for Well-Intentioned People of Pallor

YOU CAN
KEEP
THAT TO
YOURSELF

Adam Smyer

BROOKLYN, NEW YORK

Published by Akashic Books
©2020 Adam Smyer

ISBN: 978-1-61775-896-6
Library of Congress Control Number: 2020935750

All rights reserved
First printing

Printed in China

Akashic Books
Brooklyn, New York
Twitter: @AkashicBooks
Facebook: AkashicBooks
E-mail: info@akashicbooks.com
Website: www.akashicbooks.com

HELLO, WELL-INTENTIONED
PERSON OF PALLOR!

It's Daquan—the black coworker
you are referring to when you claim
to have black friends.

You are reading this book because
you want to know what not to say.
They get mad at you when you say
the wrong thing. But no one will
tell you, up front, what not to say.
Well, I will tell you. Because I am
your friend. Your real black friend.

I will tell you what not to *say*, but I will not tell you what not to *think*. Think whatever you like.

Let's review.

THOUGHTS are the things on the In side of your head. They are invisible. Your thoughts are yours. No one else's. No one else wants them.

WORDS are the things that exit your hole to the Out side of your head, where we are. They are a lot like thoughts, except that we can hear them. We don't want most of those, either. You can keep them.

Here is every word that you should keep to yourself.

Well-intentioned people of pallor went seamlessly from not seeing color to being allies. Being part of the problem was never considered. And, really, "ally" was fine for a while. It was aspirational. But now "I'm an ally" is the "Don't hurt me!" of our time. Don't nobody want you, Karen. You can keep that to yourself.

ANGRY

———

Whenever yet another white person murders a black person on video and doesn't even get in trouble, the first thing you ask me is, *Why are you so angry?* Keep that to yourself, or say what you mean: *How did you notice that we are killing you?*

———

ARTICULATE

———————

Wow! you think to yourself. *This black man talking to me is so artic-ulate!* You mean it as a compliment.

You can keep that to yourself. That black man is the judge in your DUI trial. Maybe let your lawyer do the talking.

———————

Don't speak Ebonics to us. Don't try to speak what you believe to be our language. Don't say, "They be like." Say, "They're all like," like a normal person. Keep that "be" shit to yourself.

BOTH SIDES

———

You like to say that the truth is always somewhere in the middle. You might even believe it. But that could only be true if one side isn't lying.

I know that I am a human being. The other side suggests that I am not. You want to split the baby.

Fuck the other side, and fuck you. Keep that "both sides" shit to yourself.

———

A
B
C
D
E
F
G
H
I
J
K
L
M
N
O
P
Q
R
S
T
U
V
W
X
Y
Z

CONSERVATIVE

———

Stop describing your Cousin Brett as a "conservative" to us. That's normalizing bullshit, and you can keep it to yourself.

Conservative is choosing bonds over stocks, or wearing pantyhose in the summer. That's conservative. Your Cousin Brett is a nazi.

Your cousin is a nazi.

———

DARK

———

You use light-and-dark/black-and-white imagery to signify good and evil while you are talking to me, a black person. You don't even hear yourself. Some bowl-cut translucent psycho commits a horror, and the first thing you call him is "dark." Keep us out of your fuckery.

———

ELLIS ISLAND

———

You can keep your early-20th-century European immigration story away from us. We are not impressed.

We don't care about that time some random other white person slightly shortened your grandfather's last name at Ellis Island. We weren't walking around Africa named Jeffersonetti. You know this.

Don't tell me how your grandfather came here with nothing. Some people came here with nothing; your grandfather was not among them. Your grandfather came here with not everything. He came here with less than he might have liked. Perhaps he came here with very little. So what. Getting on the boat was his idea.

See how I keep looking over your shoulder and saying "Oh wow" while you talk? That means that I give not one fuck about your recent ancestor's relatively comfortable, relatively voluntary migration. Keep it to yourself.

The only exception is if your people fled full-on Nazis. Then we can talk. Your bubbe hates her some shvartzes but, if 1939 found her ass in Poland, she's in the club whether she likes me or not.

FAM

No.

FUNKY

It's sad when you tell me that some skinny white boy in a polyester suit is "funky." P-Funk is funky. Macy Gray is funky. Anybody can mimic anybody, but that's not funk.

You keep using that word. You can keep it to yourself.

GHETTO

The gentrification of the word "ghetto" is delicious irony. It sits next to "urban" in the dog-whistle drawer. Your Uncle Scott referred to the White House as a ghetto for 8 full years. You can keep that word to yourself.

If you would like to see a ghetto, follow someone home from a Kid Rock concert.

GRAND-
FATHERED
IN

Find some way to explain how we are going to get around that new regulation other than by casually evoking the state-sponsored disenfranchisement of black people that continues to this day. It's bad enough that I'm sitting in a meeting.

A
B
C
D
E
F
G
H
I
J
K
L
M
N
O
P
Q
R
S
T
U
V
W
X
Y
Z

H AIR

Do not ask to touch our hair. Do not comment on our hair. You can look at our hair. But keep your childlike wondrous observations to yourself. Hold them in like a fart.

HONKY

A
B
C
D
E
F
G
H
I
J
K
L
M
N
O
P
Q
R
S
T
U
V
W
X
Y
Z

Only honkies say honky.

———

You lying, intelligence-insulting
motherfucker.

IGNORANCE

The word "ignorance" is your great absolver, a panacea second only to white-lady tears. When three hillbillies drag a black man to death, you fall over yourself condemning their ignorance. Except, that isn't a condemnation, is it? Because ignorance is, by definition, innocent. It isn't chosen, it can't be immediately helped, and, with a little effort, it can be completely cured. That's sweet.

Obviously, evil isn't evil when it happens to us, or when you identify with the people doing it. Please keep that to yourself.

I'M NOT
A RACIST,
BUT . . .

You use "I'm not a racist" the way we used to use "Not it." Your certainty that saying it makes it so does little to conceal your God complex. Please shut the fuck up and go away immediately.

JUNETEENTH

Don't squawk "WHAT'S JUNE-
TEENTH??" every time you hear
the word. Your cluelessness is not
cute. Google "Juneteenth" sometime,
when you're alone, and maybe let
yourself feel a little embarrassed for
not already knowing.

JUST AS BAD

The only thing you love more than saying "false equivalences" is making them. That time you felt unwelcome at a cookout isn't just as bad as gerrymandering. That black-and-white photo of a "No Irish Need Apply" sign is not just as bad as white cops strangling a black man to death for no reason in the middle of the street in broad daylight on video with few or no consequences. In fact, it's the opposite of that.

KNOWWHAT-IMSAYIN'

———

See "Be."

KWANZAA

———

Do not wish me a Happy Kwanzaa
or a Joyous Kwanzaa or whatever
you read in *White Liberal Quarterly*
to say to us. Chances are I don't ob-
serve any holiday that I can remember the creation of.

———

A
B
C
D
E
F
G
H
I
J
K
L
M
N
O
P
Q
R
S
T
U
V
W
X
Y
Z

You like to pretend that racism happened a long time ago. For the sake of your comfort, you would have me believe that next week's lynchings were a long time ago. The implication being that if an event was a long time ago it is irrelevant today and need never be spoken of. OK. Oh—Happy Washington's Birthday. And Happy Fourth of July. Happy Thanksgiving. Happy Columbus Day. Merry Christmas. Remember the Alamo. I guess "never forget" is just for you.

A
B
C
D
E
F
G
H
I
J
K
L
M
N
O
P
Q
R
S
T
U
V
W
X
Y
Z

MAGICAL

Attributing magical properties to us is your childlike way of coping when we are more talented and/or better prepared than you.

You are as open to the idea that aliens built the Great Pyramid as you are to the idea that Africans did. That's insane.

MAINSTREAM

Along with "popular" and "cross-over," you use this word to soothe yourself with the idea that all culture starts with you. You appear to believe that you will cease to exist if you are not at the center of everything.

We all know better. You are too few and too weird to pass yourselves off as normal. Maybe stop shooting everybody.

MINORITIES

It's awkward, watching you comfort yourself with the insistence that you outnumber everybody else when you plainly don't. And what you seem to think that numbers would justify is concerning.

NIGGARDLY

—

NIGGLING

A
B
C
D
E
F
G
H
I
J
K
L
M
N
O
P
Q
R
S
T
U
V
W
X
Y
Z

"Niggling" is a real word. It means "causing slight but persistent annoyance, discomfort, or anxiety." It is Scandinavian and dates back to the 17th century. "Niggardly" dates back to the 16th century. It means "stingy." It too is a real word. But you can keep them both to yourself. We know what you really want to say.

Get over it. You will be fine living your life without saying two obscure-ass words because they sound too much like a totally uncool word. Leave a buffer; that's called decency. Motherfucker, I don't say "kite."

So, I'm not supposed to comment on in-progress genocide until every white man, woman, and child are all actively committing atrocities at the same time, like the last five minutes of a zombie movie? Until no fewer than literally all of you are calling the cops on your black neighbor for chewing gum in the tub? Only then can I make observations about my reality, and the reality of my entire family going back centuries? Only then? Why would I agree to that?

You know what? Maybe literally all white people.

O VER-
SENSITIVE

Y'all snap after you have been unpop-
ular for two weeks. I've been black
my whole life. In *America*. And I'm at
least functional. *I'm* oversensitive?
The record reflects otherwise.

OWNER

The head of a large money-making organization is the CEO or the Chair. Except for sports teams. You people are so obvious. Why don't you keep that to yourself.

PRONOUNCE

Don't complain to me that you don't know how to pronounce Kwame or spell Nzinga. Motherfucker, your name is Seamus O'Shaughnessy. Shut the fuck up.

(I DON'T CARE IF YOU'RE)

PURPLE

It amazes us how often you still break out the old saw about not caring if someone is green or purple. You realize, you are likening me to some nonexistent purple alien to show that you recognize my humanity. You could try to keep that to yourself.

A
B
C
D
E
F
G
H
I
J
K
L
M
N
O
P
Q
R
S
T
U
V
W
X
Y
Z

QUALIFIED

You like to say to each other that you couldn't find any "qualified" black applicants, and then nod gravely. The black woman who went to Yale somehow wasn't qualified. The black man who's been doing exactly the work you're hiring for wasn't qualified either. But the 30 identical dullards you've hired over the years all were. OK.

QUIET

Sometimes we take up space. You wish we'd be quiet. You take up space too, but that's considered normal.

Maybe you should be quiet.

R ACIST

Once upon a time, the word "racist" meant racist.

And then a racist became some sort of boogeyman that would make Steve Bannon look moderate. You would never call someone a racist no matter what they did. Like, you would have to catch someone in a Klan robe trying to light a cross with wet matches before you even considered the possibility that you were looking at an *actual racist*. And maybe not even then. (See "Ignorance.") You started calling nazis "the alt-right" at their request.

Today, "racist" means a person who

points out when racism is happening right in front of them.

You can add "racist" to the list of words you have killed this century, along with "literally" and "ironic." And you can keep it to yourself.

———

REVERSE RACISM

Your eagerness to condemn "reverse racism" suggests that the regular kind is OK. You are actually saying it out loud.

SASSY

Sassy is your go-to. You use it affectionately to describe every black woman from Serena to Michelle. But you use the same word to attack black teenage girls you feel threatened by. The projections you impose on black women and girls approach full-blown hallucinations.

A
B
C
D
E
F
G
H
I
J
K
L
M
N
O
P
Q
R
S
T
U
V
W
X
Y
Z

I come from regular people who were abducted by evil people. I don't know who these "slaves" are.

You like that word too much. It is creepy.

SLAVERY

———

Wypipo love calling everything slavery. You call Mondays slavery. You call decaf slavery. That's called revisionism, and you can keep it.

Millions of people worked to death and worse for centuries, legally. When even one little white girl is abducted, they catch the guy and throw him under the jail, and then they pass a whole new law that makes whatever he did even more illegal, and they name the law after that poor girl.

———

THUG

Half the people you think are thugs are in high school. Meanwhile, you politely overlook the several overt nazis you pass on the street each day.

If you rounded up the ten worst mass shooters of the century, it would look like your living room on Super Bowl Sunday.

You wouldn't know a thug if one audited your taxes. Fuck outa here with that shit.

UNIVERSAL

See "Mainstream."

A
B
C
D
E
F
G
H
I
J
K
L
M
N
O
P
Q
R
S
T
U
V
W
X
Y
Z

When you describe someone as "uppity," regardless of that person's race, you sound exactly like some Klansman sheriff on his way to go lynch somebody. Which should not surprise you. You got that word from your Cousin Brett, the nazi.

VOTED
FOR
OBAMA

I'm not gonna lie—there was a time when that meant something. The good old days. But, obviously, that one act was not enough to save the country from itself. So if the last time you respected a black person was 2012, probably you should keep that to yourself.

WATERMELON

Just kidding—you can say watermelon.

A
B
C
D
E
F
G
H
I
J
K
L
M
N
O
P
Q
R
S
T
U
V
W
X
Y
Z

lol

WOMEN

"Women and minorities" means that all women are white. I know you believe that but, please, keep it to yourself.

When all you mean is white women, say so. I'm not allowed to say the words "white women," but you are.

Given your obsession with majorities, going forward when I hear you say "women" I am going to assume you mean Asian women.

Don't quote Malcolm X to black people. Don't quote Malcolm X to white
people. Don't quote Malcolm X to
Latino people.

Don't quote Malcolm X.

Y'ALL
—
Yo

———————

See "Be."

Southern white people seem to come by
their "y'all"s honestly, albeit violently.

———————

A
B
C
D
E
F
G
H
I
J
K
L
M
N
O
P
Q
R
S
T
U
V
W
X
Y
Z

Y OU'RE
DIFFERENT

———

No I'm not. I'm different from what your mama told you I was, when you were a baby. Your mama lied to you.

———

A
B
C
D
E
F
G
H
I
J
K
L
M
N
O
P
Q
R
S
T
U
V
W
X
Y
Z

———

It's weird—one minute we are having a normal conversation, and the next you are blurting out a minstrel show catchphrase. Verbal blackface.

So inappropriate! But mostly just weird. A thought: you could not.

———

A
B
C
D
E
F
G
H
I
J
K
L
M
N
O
P
Q
R
S
T
U
V
W
X
Y
Z

ZEBRA

It can be uncomfortable to listen to you work out your racial distress in real time. Particularly when, as is often the case, you seem to take the concept of color literally. (See also "Purple.")

Your metaphors are endless (striped African equids, piano keys, cookies, etc.) and troubling. If you need to do thought experiments in order not to be triggered by the actual sight of me, like some pumpkin-spiced George Zimmerman, then, by all means, do them. But maybe keep them to yourself?

My concern isn't so much your light-

pink skin as it is all the violence,
and your being pretty OK with all
the violence.

ZEPPELIN

You like Led Zeppelin because they are white people playing black music. If you were older, you would have an Al Jolson T-shirt collection instead. (See also the Black Crowes and the Black Keys, which together include zero black people.)

Those of us who can bear hearing black music played by black people don't need Zeppelin. They are hacks. Feel free to keep them to yourself.

There it is. Every word you can keep to your damn self.

There is so, so much that you *can* say. If we are at work, you can talk about work. (It really would be great if you could only talk to us about work, but we understand that you don't know where you are.) You can talk about the weather and/or sports. You can talk about your favorite shows. You can even talk about current events if your family raised you properly.

But.

When you are talking to a black
person and you suddenly *remember* that you are talking to a black
person. And that *a black person is
talking to you.* When your yogic
not-color-seeing trance slips and it
hits you, fresh.

We see it on your face. Your real-
time awareness of interacting with
an actual full-on **BLACK PERSON**
kicks in and becomes too much
for you, and you feel compelled to
speak on it. You *must*, you think.
Your eyes take on a mad gleam.
You struggle to find words fitting
for this occasion.

We are standing there, looking into
your wild eyes and pulling for you
to keep it all the fuck to yourself.

It's weird when people want to kill you and fuck you and be you. But that's just the way it is. It's bigger than me and it's bigger than you. It will never change. But maybe you could stop telling me?

You can do it!

I hope this helps!

Really, really hope this helps!

Thanks for reading, WIPOP! You can and should say literally everything else you want to say, to whomever you want to say it. And please keep dropping my name every chance you get.

See you at work!

~Daquan